Guide to CNC Sign Making

If you're a CNC hobbyist or crafter who would like to make signs you've probably learned that the machining part is EASY. The hard part is designing and finishing great looking signs. You need help.

You've come to the right place. This book will lead you through the sign making process with simple non-technical language and show you many examples of great signs made by people just like you. Sign making isn't rocket science, you simply need to learn a few practical techniques and design basics to start producing eye-catching signs on your CNC.

You'll learn about layout and design basics, font choices, creating and using sign shapes, various sign styles, choosing materials, tool selection, production methods, and finishing techniques.

Dedicated to Jim Hester

My friend, confidant, editor-without-pay, good-natured sounding board, candid critic, and well-rounded human being. He's been with me since the beginning of this CNC journey, and there's no telling what we might accomplish if he didn't live so far away.

With special thanks to these talented sign makers for the use of their photos:

Cade Banks

Leigh Ann Bishop

Talley-Shauna Boatwright

Paul D. Bond

Don Brown, Jr.

Justin Carr

Teresa Carson

Branwen Cole

Lee Cowan

Grant Davis

Zack Donahue

Patrick Eaton

Richard Gonzalez

Wayne Gnagey

Jason Herrman

Jim Hester

Mike Taubitz and Joanne Hibbert

Stacy Hines

Cris Hinojosa

Tom Hollander

Dustin Henry Horton

Robert Howells

Bobbie Lewis

Katie and Jason Lovejoy

Christine Kirby Rock-Ellis

Kerri Kershaw Niemeyer

Eddie Nowak

Robert Peloat

Paul A. Pomeroy

Casey Reames

Jeff Schumacher

Travis Scott

Ricky Shafer

Brady Travis

David Tolley

Stephen Taylor

Rob and Vanessa Tremblay

Trevor Viner

Justin Walsh

Bob Mary Walters

Gary Wiant

Paul E. Wilson

Allen Yarberry

Darrick Vanderford

Contents

Section 2 Production Styles & Techniques 28

Section 3 Finishing Techniques 58

Design and Layout

What's the hardest part about making signs? It isn't the software. The CAD/CAM software available to us, like Vectric's V Carve and Aspire, have a full range of drawing tools to combine text, art, and shapes to make a wide variety of signs from wood, foam, acrylic, plastic, and even metal. Add painting and finishing into the mix, and you'll have a great looking sign.

Other software like Inkscape, Corel Draw, and Adobe Illustrator are excellent for designing and laying out signs.

And, if you find it difficult working on the computer screen to think through a design, there's always the tried and true method of sketching ideas with pencil and paper.

A good layout is the key to every successful sign.

Regardless of how you approach sign making, it all starts with an idea and a design.

But design is the big stumbling block, isn't it? The software can help, but we have to tell it what to do. And, we're not all talented graphic designers and artists.

Here's the good news: You don't need all those special design skills. You just need to follow some simple design principles to start making eye-catching signs.

If you need ideas, just look around. Ideas for sign designs are all around you, and there's nothing wrong with copying a style you like and changing it to match your needs.

Even if you're starting from scratch, you can create pleasing layouts for visually appealing signs without agonizing over all the details. You just need some text, a shape for your sign, and maybe some artwork.

It's merely a question of how to arrange all those elements to make an effective and attractive sign. Some simple guidelines will make that easier.

Let's get started.

Working with text

The text seems like the easiest part of the layout. After all, you've got all those fonts on your PC to choose from, right? What can go wrong?

Every typeface causes an emotion in the viewer, and they are subconsciously affected by it. Is your font warm and friendly, or more serious and formal? Your font needs to match the intent of the sign, or the viewer finds it disconcerting.

A formal font doesn't work where the viewer expects a more casual approach ...

Playtime Daycare Center
Playtime Daycare Center

... any more than a casual font should be used for a serious message.

In Memory of John Smith
In Memory of John Smith

Many sign carvers use only one font, Times Roman, for the text on ALL their signs. Most of the time, it fails to work with the sign's intended message.

Just as a side note. Many graphic designers think Times Roman should NEVER be used for anything. It was developed in the early

BASIC FONT STYLES

SERIF

TRADITIONAL | CLASSIC | FASHIONABLE

SAN-SERIF

MODERN | CLEAN | CASUAL

FEMININE | CREATIVE | FRIENDLY

CONDENSED

BOLD | STRONG | MODERN

ROUNDED

SOFT | CHILDLIKE | FRIENDLY

CARTOON

FUN | FRIENDLY | CASUAL

chart concept from ForthAndCreate.com

1900s to fit narrow newspaper columns and was definitely never intended as a headline or display font, which how many are using it for the major words on their signs.

Let's call this our first Rule of Thumb:

1. Be sure the font matches the message.

See? Easy to understand and easy to remember.

Now let's get back to all those fonts we have. We want our sign to have visual variety and contrast so why not use more than one font? Anything we need to worry about there?

Yes. Nothing says amateur designer more than mixing a wide variety of fonts.

When you use too many fonts on one sign it ends up looking like a ransom note rather than a sign. Just because you have all those fonts, doesn't mean they should all be used at the same time.

A good design limits the number of fonts to two, or at the most three.

Let's make that our second rule of thumb:

2. Use no more than two fonts on your sign.

Now let's talk about mixing and matching fonts. When done poorly, you end up with

what at best is a confusing sign, and at the worst an ugly one.

You can see the basic styles of type in the side panel on the previous page. The list is just a high-level overview. There many sub-styles in each of those categories.

3. Choose fonts that work together.

Our third Rule is to choose font pairs carefully. Serif fonts work with sans serif, and script fonts work with serif and sans serif. However, two script fonts seldom work well together.

Also, avoid pairing fonts that are too similar. Text needs contrast, and with fonts that look too much alike, any small differences tend to look like a mistake.

4. Space text carefully.

Word and letter spacing is an essential part of making a sign that looks visually correct to the viewer.

Accurately spaced type is less of a problem when you are using the computer to set a line of type. But when you are combining two or more words that weren't set at the same time, spacing may be an issue. Generally, words are spaced about the width of the letter "i."

Wordsiareispacedi theiwidthiofitheiletteri"i"
Words are spaced the width of the letter "i"

This is not a hard and fast rule, but it's a helpful way to check when you're not sure if your word spacing looks right.

Kerning is also important. Kerning is adjusting the space between letters. In print, letters in headlines are often kerned, so they are closer together.

The large text on our signs may be considered a headline, but remember we aren't putting type on paper, we're carving text into our material.

Closely spaced letters can work if we're just v-carving the text. Carving around the letters is a different story because we need extra space between the letters to allow room for the size of the tool.

Here's the same text carved both inset and outset using a 60º v-bit. Wider letter spacing was needed for the outset text.

5. Some fonts are problems

This rule is to remind us that not all fonts are suitable for CNC work.

Remember, the fonts on your computer were designed, and intended, for print, not our CNC machines.

This Pirates Bay font looks very cool in print.

Pirates Bay

But look what happens when we use it in our CAD program and check the nodes. Each dot is a node, and every letter has an exceedingly high number of them which will

cause very jerky machining motions, and significantly increase the carving time.

It's a good idea to examine the nodes (Node Edit in Vectric's V Carve) with an unfamiliar font to be sure it will cut efficiently.

Script fonts have their own issues

This is really a production issue rather than a design and layout issue, but it's mentioned here so you don't end up wondering why you can't get your beautiful sign layout to carve correctly.

While script fonts print perfectly, and may even v-carve correctly, the overlapping vectors can cause problems with some tool paths.

To avoid problems, it's a good practice to convert the text to curves or outlines and use a merge or unite tool to eliminate the overlapping vectors.

The toolpath problems will be eliminated and your sign will carve just as you expected.

We'll talk more about script fonts when we get into making Stacked Text signs.

That's the end of our Text Rules of Thumb. Five simple, easy-to-remember, and easy to use guidelines to help you make better signs.

Next, let's talk about using graphics.

Working with graphics

You already know this, but it's essential to review it — just in case. In the design world, there are two types of graphics files, bitmaps, and vectors.

Bitmap images are stored as a series of fixed-size tiny dots called pixels. These files are digital photos or scanned images with file extensions like gif, bmp, png, tiff, and jpeg. Enlarging a bitmap merely enlarges the size of the pixels, and the graphic can lose detail quickly.

Vector images, on the other hand, are not based on pixel patterns. Vectors use mathematical formulas to draw lines and curves that can be combined to create an image. Vector images have file extensions such as eps, svg, ai, pdf, and dxf. Vector files can be scaled up or down to any size without losing any detail since their shape is defined by mathematics.

Remember what CNC means? Computer Numerically Controlled. Numerical is the keyword, and why we need to use vectors to create our toolpaths.

Bitmap Graphic

Vector Graphic

Converting bitmaps

There are some options if your graphic is a bitmap instead of a vector. Software like Adobe Illustrator, Inkscape, Magic Tracer, and Corel Draw have tracing tools that will trace your bitmap and convert it to vectors. A quick search will also lead you to some online resources for creating vectors.

Adobe Illustrator is probably the program that most graphic designers use for illustration, and it has a well-rounded bitmap tracing function.

Adobe Illustrator bitmap conversion

Vectric's V Carve CAD/CAM program also has a bitmap tracing function. And, while it doesn't have as many options as Illustrator, it allows you to fine-tune your bitmap-to-vector conversions.

Which one is best? As you can see from the images on the right, the two conversions look virtually the same. One minor difference is that the Illustrator file has slightly fewer nodes than the V Carve file, which might make a somewhat smoother tool path.

Vectric V Carve bitmap conversion

There are many online sources where you can find and download a wide variety of vector-formatted graphics. For example, a search for "black and white butterfly" on **vectorstock.com** revealed 5,400 images.

Integrating graphics with text

Just slapping an image on your layout for the sake of having one isn't the way to design a sign. Too often, sign makers stick an image in the corner of the sign, and it ends up looking like a wallflower at a dance.

The graphic should integrate with the text to unify the sign and make it attractive to the viewer.

There is an old graphic design rule of thumb that a person in a photo should look into the page, not out of it, to draw the eye into the headline and text.

We sign makers need to practice this also. Here's an example of a simple sign with an appropriate graphic.

But, in the first example of this simple sign layout, notice how it feels like the kneeling fireman is turning his back on the message, and he's drawing our eye away from it.

In the second layout, he is looking into the sign and leading our eyes to the message, making him a cohesive part of the design.

Yes, it seems like a trivial matter, but the subtle difference makes a sign that is more appealing to the viewer.

Support our
First Responders
who risk everything

Support our
First Responders
who risk everything

Usually, our sign layouts start with content, like the customer's name, rather than an image. Then most of us start looking for a font that we like, and after experimenting with what seems like a bazillion, we finally choose one.

Salty's Marina
Boat Slip Rentals

Okay, we've got a font, and we're feeling good, so let's find some clip art that might work. It's a marina, so it needs to be something nautical. How about a ship's wheel? Hey, there's an anchor. Let's use that too.

Cool. We're done, right? Maybe not. Signs need contrast to be effective. Our layout has all the text the same size, and with the images, it looks like one solid block of color. Squint at it, and you'll get the idea.

The first fix is to avoid visual monotony by changing the size of the second line of type to create contrast between the lines of text.

Now, here's another essential design rule. One image is always more powerful than two. Every image you add dilutes the others.

By eliminating the extra image, reshuffling our layout, and integrating the graphic, we can come up with a pretty good looking sign.

Travis Scott's beach sign is an excellent example of how simple it is to integrate the art with the text for a unified, eye-catching design that feels right to the viewer.

Think about how it would look without the circle cutting into the text. The palm trees would be isolated at the side, looking lost and lonely.

Using text as a graphic

Sometimes text alone can be an effective graphic, especially with some of the fancier fonts.

The **MFC Elmstead Monogram** font collection gives a variety of ways to create personalized signage with little effort. For the split letter versions, there is a small-caps font that is perfectly sized to fit inside the split and make it easy to add text.

An Internet search for monogram vectors will turn up graphics like the Vintage Capital Letter Monograms from vectorstock.com, used on the Hester sign. **The vector letters come in two sets, A—L, and M—Z.**

Another popular option is to use just the word itself as art. Obviously, this works best with a script or other connected font. This word art by **Richard Gonzalez** is an excellent example. We'll talk about this style of sign in detail later.

sign by Travis Scott

MFC Elmstead font

sign by Prof. Henry

word art by Richard Gonzalez

Using borders and frames

Another option for quickly designing a sign is to use vector shapes and frames. Often you can use them as-is, although you can always modify them to suit your needs.

For example, **Letterheadfonts. com** has a series of vintage style frames that are actually a font. This is the letter Z from their **Broadway Panels 1** collection. It lends itself to a beautiful looking vintage sign on its own, but it is easy to modify.

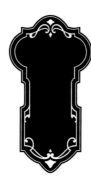

The panel made by this letter looks like it has good potential, but we need to modify it before we can use it by converting it to outlines.

We'll also simplify the panel by removing some of the outer vectors, and rotating it 180º because it feels a little top-heavy. Now the wider portion gives us a solid base.

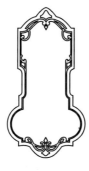

We're getting there, but we still need a few modifications. The central area is too short for our text, so we need to stretch it to move the top section up until there is room for the text.

One last step and we can add the rest of our text and art.

Our art needs more space at the top, so let's chop off the top and add a few circles to create a frame and border. Of course, we'll have to fiddle around connecting the circles and existing borders, but that's an easy task in V Carve or any other vector drawing app. The circle helps balance the heavy-feeling bottom.

When we add the rest of our art and text, we have a design ready for toolpaths, carving, and finishing.

Yes, there was some extra work required to make the sign layout, but using the font/shape gave us a head start, and simplified our design process.

Here's another example, where the font shape was used with no modification other than adding some artwork and text. This shape is the numeral **7** in **Letterheadfonts. com's Broadway Panels 4** collection.

As you can see, it was easy to make a vintage-looking sign without trying to draw shapes and create flourishes. The only drawing required was the gear and the bottom text panel. Both were created in Vectric's V Carve Pro.

There are a lot of design resources that will save you time and headaches as you think through and layout your sign.

Always take advantage of anything that can shorten the design process because you'll find that you spend more time on design then you do actually making something on the CNC.

Here's a 20-minute sign design that started with a clip art eagle from **Vectorstock.com.** A search on the site showed there were over 4,500 options, but this was one of the first to pop up and looked like it would v-carve well.

The eagle vector was imported into V Carve, and all the layout was done there. The result is a sign that can be carved with only two bits, a 90º v-bit for the eagle, text, border,

and edge chamfer. Then a 1/4" spiral end mill to cut out the outline. The carving is about a 10—15-minute job on the CNC.

So, not counting finishing, this project took less than an hour to make. That's the beauty of using some of the art sources available on the Internet.

A word of caution.

Do not use copyrighted logos like those from the sports and entertainment industry, if you are selling your product.

There are plenty of royalty-free art sources, and the last thing you want is a visit from angry lawyers.

Sign shapes

We've seen some different ways to use text and graphics to make a good sign layout, and we've seen how some graphics actually work well as a sign shape.

Once again, it's time to **"think outside the box."** In this case, we're talking about the boxy, square, or rectangular sign. Sure there are a lot of great looking signs like that, but we want our signs to go beyond the ordinary.

Giving shape to your sign adds visual dimension and makes it appear more prestigious.

Look how the shape of **Eddie Nowak's** sign draws the eye right to the dog image, and then opens wider for the text. The double border adds another element that ties it all together.

Rob and Vanessa Tremblay used the large monogram as the basis of the sign shape. Everything wraps around the text and gives it a sense of formality that wouldn't be present if the sign was merely carved in a rectangular space.

Don't shy away from adding shape to your sign because you think it's too hard to design, and you need some pre-made vectors. It's easier than you think.

sign by Eddie Nowak

sign by Rob &Vanessa Tremblay - The Knotty Carver
facebook.com/theknottycarver5

Let's walk through creating a sign shape
Here's how the Salty's Marina sign shape evolved using only simple basic shapes.

1 First a rectangle was drawn around the main headline and bars. The size was arbitrary, and just looked right visually.

2 Next a circle was drawn centered on the ships wheel, and a smaller rectangle was drawn around the bottom line of text.

3 Since the shapes looked bland, inset corners were added to the large box, and rounded corners added to the small.

4 Next using one of design's handiest tools, the basic shapes were all merged into one, giving a nice shape for the sign.

5 Finally, it was a simple matter of creating a new outline by offsetting the merged shape to create the final border.

As you can see, you can easily create a shape for your sign no matter what your skill level.

Let the content define the shape

Sometimes the content of the sign suggests the shape, and in most cases, it is the perfect shape to use.

Paul Pomeroy's police badge is a simple v-carved sign rather than a detailed, long-to-produce 3D carve. And yet, making the sign the shape of the badge yields added dimension, and gives the viewer the sense of a 3D sign.

sign by Paul A. Pomeroy

Robert Howell used the same technique for his Marine Corps Special Operations Command insignia. Once again, it is a simple v-carve, and matching the shape to the content gives it a tangible sense of the badge. It would be less dynamic if it were merely carved into a rectangular shape.

Perhaps the shapes **Justin Carr** used for his word signs are a no-brainer, but they still enhance the final result. The background shapes for the Ethan and Emma signs only loosely follow the letter shapes, and yet feel like they are the exact shape of the words.

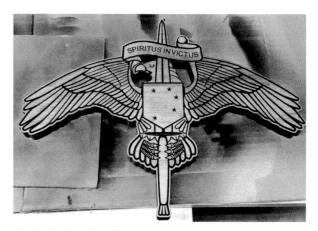

Sign by Robert Howells

Learn to open your mind while working on your sign layout to see if the content suggests a shape.

Sometimes if you step back to view your design from a distance, and squint, a shape becomes readily apparent, and it may be the best solution for that sign.

signs by Justin Carr

Some basic sign shapes

Here are some common sign shapes you may want to use. However, don't underestimate the power of simple.

Dustin Henry Horton's cleanly designed logo is given an extra touch of sophistication with the simple oval shape of the sign.

sign by Dustin Henry Horton

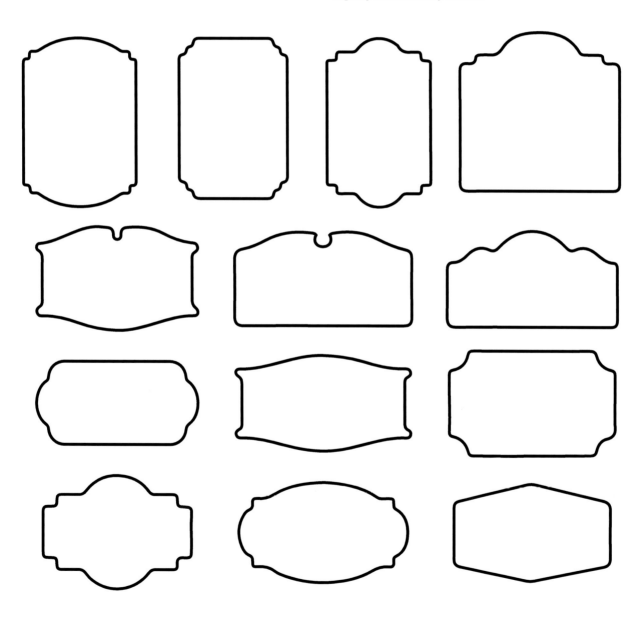

sign by Brady Travis - Travis Custom Woodworks

sign by Michael Taubitz and Joanne Hibbert
Mike's Custom Unusual

By ignoring the constraints of boxy shapes, and letting your text or artwork escape the shape's boundary, your signs can quickly move to an exciting new level. Let's look at some examples so you can see how a simple sign can be moved from Ho-Hum to Wow!

Brady Travis skillfully let the R and E in his Rust-eze sign escape the border of a round sign. Combined with the slanted text, it gives the sign a feeling of movement and power. Pocketing the majority of the text to make it raised, combined with the v-carved text in the extended leg of the R adds more dimension. If everything was constrained inside the circle, the sign would be less vibrant.

Michael Taubitz and Joanne Hibbert took a similar approach with their Brettwood sign by letting the company name and the saw blade break free of the basic rectangular shape. Looking closely, you can see the sign is a simple v-carve, which if it were just within a rectangle shape, would be far less memorable..

Stephen Taylor used a basic sign shape and then added the flowers to one corner, letting them expand off the edge. While his sign was already 2.5-D, extending beyond the boundary added a new level of interest.

Sign by Stephen Taylor

Why does the word "dimension" keep popping up?

Most of the signs you see every day are flat. When you make your sign dimensional, you add shadows and texture, which dramatically increase the sign's eye appeal.

It's easy to think outside the box once you learn the concept.

Let's take a look at the evolution of a simple project. We're going to make a visitor's center and gift shop sign for the Windchime Gardens, and we want to add a butterfly to the sign.

Since this will be a simple v-carved sign, we'll use some vector clip art for the butterfly.

Now let's start laying out our sign. Naturally, we'll start with a basic sign shape, and add some text.

Next, we need to add our clip art butterfly to the mix to see how it looks. Let's size it to match the height of the capital letters in the name and align it with the text.

Well, that's okay but still kind of boring. How about if we inset the corners to make the shape a little more engaging?

Better, but it's still pretty blah. **Time to think outside the box and make a bold change.** Let's make the butterfly a lot bigger, and put it at an angle to give it some movement.

There it is! That's all it takes to add some real interest to a simple v-carved sign, where the text and art can be carved with a 90º v-bit.

6 Quick Ways to improve your designs and take your signs to the next level.

1. Add Contrast and establish a hierarchy by changing font sizes and add a contrasting font. Curving text adds interest and a sense of movement.

2. Change from the boring rectangle by putting your design inside a simple shape to add more contrast.

3. Add a border by expanding the shape outward to give your sign a more stable and finished look.

4. Add dimension, depth, and shadow by pocketing the background to create raised text and artwork.

5. Add a texture, to enhance your sign and give it a sense of higher style and perceived value.

6. Burst out of the box and add visual interest by extending parts of your design beyond the boundaries of the shape.

Experiment with your sign designs in your drawing and CAD program, or even on paper with pen or pencil.

Don't get fixated on your first idea. Change sizes, shapes, and positions. Move things around. Switch from horizontal to vertical format.

Keep working at it until the final sign looks right. Squint at your designs to get a feel for how the elements blend together and what the sign might look like from a distance.

The more you play with your designs, the more you learn, and the design process becomes more natural.

Design and Layout ■ **27**

Production
Styles & Techniques

Often while working on the design and layout of a sign, we haven't thought about how we're going to carve it on the CNC. Or, if we have, we're disappointed with the tool path preview and want to make a change.

A planned simple v-carve might look better as a pocketed 2.5-D carve, and vice versa, we might find a 2.5-D carve takes too long for quick production of generic signs.

Each style has its own advantages and weaknesses, along with the techniques of how to produce them. Let's take a look at those now.

Cutout and stacked Word Signs

Cutout word signs are popular with both customers and sign makers. They are quick and easy to design and cut, and require minimal finishing, making them an ideal project.

word art by Richard Gonzalez

Some sign makers cut the word art and sell it as a stand-alone product. The word art by **Richard Gonzalez** is an excellent example of how well a stand-alone word sign looks.

Others like **Justin Carr** place it on a carved background for support and making it both literally and visually more substantial.

sign by Justin Carr
Shore Thing Custom Woodworks

Word art is generally cut from 1/2"—3/4" MDF or Baltic Birch plywood, using a 1/8" or 1/4" spiral end mill, cutting outside the letter vectors. Using a down-cut spiral bit will leave a smooth surface on the top while causing tear out on the bottom, and the upcut spiral bit will do the reverse.

Compression bit photo © Amana Tool Co.

Richard cuts his word art out of 1/2" Baltic Birch plywood with either a 1/4" or 1/8" compression bit. Compression bits have both up-cut and down-cut spiral flutes especially designed to eliminate tearing or chipping on both surfaces. The upcut flutes at the tip of a compression bit are approximately 1/3 the overall cutting length.

He uses two passes (the first deep enough to bury the upcut portion of the bit), with .005" allowance for last pass cleanup, so no lines appear on the profile cuts. He finds it better to cut the holes inside any of the letters before cutting the final outline.

The compression bit packs the kerf with chips, and Richard finds they work as well as tabs, to prevent the cut words from moving, and the lack of tabs requires less post-carving cleanup.

Cutouts can be fragile, with the thin sections being very flexible, which is why they are often attached to a backer.

Branwen Cole works in collaboration with **Richard Gonzalez** and uses his CNC cutouts to make her signs. She assembled old, aged fence wood for her round sign, and cut it using a jigsaw with a fine blade. Three cross supports are attached to the back.

Cutting shapes like that out of irregular material is often faster and easier with regular tools instead of the CNC.

The words are glued to the backing with regular wood glue and also tacked in place with 18 ga brads or 23ga pin nails.

Leigh Ann Bishop used a similar technique. Her multi-layered sign adds more dimension and increases the shadows for effective contrast against the stained background.

sign by Branwen Cole
On the Wall Designs

sign by Leigh Ann Bishop
Bishop Woodworking - Facebook

The technique of cutting out and stacking design elements isn't limited to just words alone. **Ricky Shafer** embraced the mid-century retro look for these great looking cut and stacked signs.

All of the shapes and text are cut on the CNC and then assembled into one unit. Using profile toolpaths for each of the elements, he cuts them out of the plywood with a 1/8" bit to ensure the fine details are maintained.

The backing layers are 1/2" birch plywood to add stability, and the text and decorations are cut from 1/4" birch plywood.

Baltic Birch plywood is preferable for all signs of this type because it has about double the number of plies found in most other plywoods and generally is void-free. The additional plies add the stiffness and stability needed for the potentially fragile cutouts.

Glue up is done carefully using a brush to apply slightly thinned PVA glue (Titebond III - waterproof when dry). Glue squeeze-out can be cleaned up with a damp Q-tip.

Ricky paints each piece with rattle-can spray paint before assembly. The entire sign receives a clear coat of matte finish after assembly.

The cut and stacked technique is an easy way to build up dimensional signs, and the individual elements simplify painting and finishing.

signs by Ricky Shafer - Blue Sky Mayhem

V Carved Signs

Don't underestimate what you can do with a basic 60º or 90º v-bit. V-carving is one of the most efficient toolpaths, and there are countless sign carvers producing signs every day using only this tool.

V-carved signs give you the most bang-for-the-buck of all the sign carving techniques. They are quick to produce, easy to finish, have universal appeal, and it's easy to translate your artwork into a finished sign. Some makers crank out 10 to 12 v-carved signs a day.

Generally, you don't have to set the depth of cut for a V-carve toolpath because the depth is determined by v-bit's angle and the width of the vectors.

When you put a funnel into the neck of a bottle, it can go in only so far before the angle of the funnel's sides makes it wider than the opening and prevents it from going any deeper into the bottle.

The vector outlines of the letters and art are like the bottle opening, and the V-bit is like the angled sides of the funnel. The bit can only carve down until it hits the vectors that are the edges of the art and text.

Sign by Prof. Henry

Sign by Gary Wiant

Router bit photo © Whiteside Machine Co.

As and example of how easy it is to make a v-carved sign, the **Hester** sign was carved using only a 90º v-bit for both the text and the border.

Here are some checkpoints to make sure you get the best v-carve:

- Make sure your material is flat. If it's not, the depth of your carve may vary from one area to another. (Look carefully at the Hester sign, and you can see that the second name is carved slightly less deep than the first name.)

- The table needs to be level, and the bit perfectly perpendicular to it, or you will have the same depth issues.

- Set the Z-axis accurately to the top of the material.

- Keep your bits sharp for clean cuts.

- Check your tool if your v-carves don't look quite right. You may find the angle of your bit isn't what it says. A 90º bit may actually be 89º or 91º.

When carving large letters, or graphics, the width of the vectors may be wider than your bit which would cause it to cut all the way through your stock.

In that case, you need to use either a v-bit with a wider angle or set a depth of cut for the toolpath. With a depth of cut setting, you may want to add a flat area clearance tool, such as a 1/8" end mill to clear the bulk of the material inside the vectors.

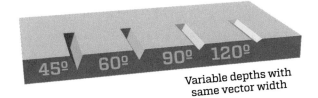

Variable depths with same vector width

Gary Wiant cleverly took advantage of the curved border and tree leaves to cut the shape around the deer artwork and used the banner at the bottom for the large Welcome text. A very eye-catching sign made from pine and done with basic v-carve toolpaths.

Bobbie Lewis' sign shows a technique that dramatically speeds up v-carved sign production. By painting the material's surface before carving, the material's color shows through after carving and gives all the contrast needed for a highly readable sign, and only requires a clear finishing coat.

Sign by Bobbie Lewis

Kerri Kershaw Niemeyer used a combination of a v-bit and straight bit to carve the general contractor sign.

Kerri's sign is also an excellent example of integrating artwork with the text to create a crisp, well-balanced, and unified design.

Christine Kirby Rock Ellis' simple v-carve jumps to a new level of visual appeal by merely cutting out the shape of the state. It's still a flat sign, but the instantly identifiable shape adds arresting dimension that any sports fan could recognize from across a room.

Many CNCers make more v-carved signs than any other type because they are fast and easy to design, carve, and finish. We'll talk more about finishing later on.

The Hester sign we talked about earlier was a 15-minute carve. Most of the signs you've seen in this section would carve in about the same time. That's the beauty of v-carved signs — fast production. Something that is important when you are making a large quantity of signs for sales at craft shows and fairs, or through an online market place.

If you set up your CAD files correctly, you can have a template where you only need to change information to add personalization.

sign by Kerri Kershaw Niemeyer

sign by Christine-Kirby Rock-Ellis

Use templates for fast v-carve production

What happens when you need to make a large number of signs—for instance, address signs for a subdivision—that must conform to a set standard, but each requires different information? Your time at the computer could take as long as your time on the CNC.

This is where CAD/CAM apps like Vectric's V Carve and Aspire can simplify the task by making it easy to set up templates.

Follow along while we set up a file to make a series of signs out of 6" x 18" x 3/4" stock. We know each sign must have a name and address that fits uniformly inside a border.

Layers are the key to making a template where toolpaths can be quickly created for changeable information. We'll use one layer for the name and address, and another for the border.

This next step isn't necessary, but for our project, we'd like the name to fill the same amount of space inside the border on every sign, so we'll draw a box for the name, sized to fit within that boundary.

To set up the Name text we'll use the **Auto Layout Text** option in V Carve.

This option automatically sizes a block of text to fit inside the bounding box (width and height limits) of a selected vector.

Font: TrueType / Single Line — Sancreek abcdeABCDE

Bold / Italic

Text Alignment: Left / Center / Right

Bounding Box Dimensions:
Width: 16.0 inches
Height: 2.6669 inches

Margin Size: None / Normal / Wide

Vertical Stretch: Stretch Characters

Horizontal Stretch: Stretch Characters

While setting the width and height of the box, we also choose to vertically and horizontally stretch the text to fit. The address text can be set normally because it can have a variable length.

Here's how our layout looks. The red box is the text box, which will not be used for calculating toolpaths.

We'll setup basic v-carve toolpaths using a 90º v-bit for the text and border. The name and address can be combined into one toolpath. No tool changes will be needed.

Here's where our quick-change template trick comes into play.

Before calculating the text v-carve tool path, we need to use the **Vector Selection** option.

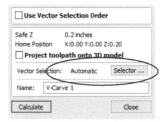

The dialog box that opens allows us to **Associate the Vectors** (our text) with the toolpath. This means

that whenever we recalculate our toolpaths, it will v-carve whatever is on the selected layer, which in our case are the changeable name and address.

Creating toolpaths for the multitude of signs is a simple 4-step process: type the name in the name box, type the address, use the re-calculate toolpaths button, and save the two paths (text and border) to a single g-code file. About a 1-minute process for each sign.

You can also save time in the shop by preparing all your stock to a uniform size in advance, and setting up your CNC so you can quickly place the material in precisely the same position for each carve. If done correctly, you can set your X, Y axes once and use the setting for every sign. Production is fast. Place a blank on the table, double-check the Z axis, select the proper file, and carve. Keep repeating the process until all the signs are completed.

Each name fits inside the border the same way on every sign regardless of length.

A positioning jig for your CNC table simplifies repeat operations.

Signs with the ultimate Wow! factor

The extra dimension added by 3-D carving can make some spectacular looking signs.

Travis Scott made the shell sign at the left using one of Vectric's tutorial files. The name added to the 3-D carved ribbon, plus the shell image, and excellent finish makes an elegant sign

Wayne Gnagey replicated a wine barrel lid complete with wine bottles and glasses plus grapes and grape leaves. Adding the personalization makes it a keepsake for the customer.

3-D signs require CAD/CAM software that can handle creating 3-D models, and outputting the required toolpaths. Programs like Fusion 3-D, Vectric Aspire, or Carveco can create the 3-D models, and programs like Vectric's V-Carve Desktop and V-Carve Pro can import and carve 3-D files created in

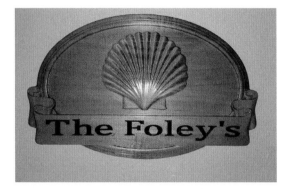

sign by Travis Scott

sign by Wayne Gnagney

sign by Prof. Henry

sign by Paul D. Bond - American Woodgrain
Facebook: Americanwoodgrain

From a production standpoint, 3-D signs take a lot more machine time—many hours—and will need to sell at a much higher price than a 2-D or 2.5-D carved sign.

The EMS sign by **Paul Bond** is 12" x 14", and he used a 1/16" ball nose bit to get the detail he needed. This carve took 10 hours to complete, which works out to about three and a half minutes per square inch.

This beautiful and detailed sign by **Stacy Hines** is an excellent example of the time required for 3-D carvings. His roughing pass with a 1/2" end mill took 14 hours, and the finishing path with a 1/4" ball nose bit took 16 hours.

another program. Learning to create a 3-D model can be a long learning curve.

An alternative to making your own 3-D files is to purchase ready-made art elements or complete models. All the artwork on the previous page were part of Vectric's clip art library or purchased from DesignandMake.com. There are many providers of 3-D files, and some will create custom designs for you based on your needs.

Unless you are producing a lot of custom 3-D work, it makes sense to purchase ready-made models. You can combine existing 3-D elements to create an entirely different look, and make your sign look like it was a custom product.

sign by Stacy Hines - Facebook: Stacey's Woodcrafts

Sign by Talley-Shauna Boatwright

Talley-Shaun Boatwright's' barber shop sign is another fantastic example of what can be done with skill, time, and talent when working in 3-D. He successfully made the new sign look like an antique that's been with the shop for decades.

So you can see that while carving 3-D signs is not fast, the results can be extraordinary, and well worth the effort.

Let's take a look at the process

3-D signs use two basic toolpaths. First, a roughing pass is done with a larger bit to hog out most of the material. The roughing pass is followed by a finishing path using a small ball nose bit to get the final depth and detail.

For this example, we're using an eagle and flag design fromVectric's DesignandMake website. Once we've placed it on our layout, sized it accordingly and centered it, we're ready to get started.

We want our finished model to sit above the surface of the sign, so we first we need to draw a rectangular vector (red line) that is 1/4" off of the

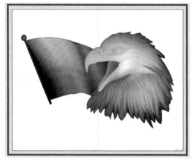

Model and outside vector

edges of the sign. The vector ensures the tools will cut away the background entirely without leaving a raised edge. Without the rectangular vector, the model would carve into the surface of the sign.

With the outside vector in place, we can move on to making our toolpaths.

The first step in making toolpaths is to double-check our material setup to be sure our 3-D model will be machined correctly.

Our stock is 3/4," and the model is 3/8" deep. The graphic shows we have a small gap above the graphic that will be cut away, and we have plenty of stock below the bottom of the model.

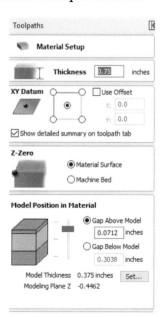

The roughing toolpath

Our first toolpath is for roughing out the bulk of the material. We'll use a 1/4" end mill for this operation. We don't need to set a depth of cut because the depth is determined by the model.

To make the path we select both the model and the outside vector we drew earlier.

You can see that the roughing pass has removed a lot of the stock with the background surface almost down to the finished level.

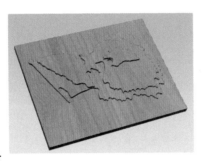

Completed roughing pass

The finishing toolpath

We'll use a 1/8" ball nose bit for finishing. Using a smaller bit would give more detail but require a much longer carving time. Part of the reason 3-D

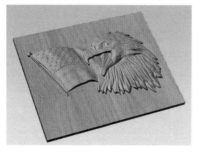

Completed finishing pass

carving takes so long is that the step-over setting for the bit is generally around 8% or less, so it is cutting very little material with each pass. A larger step-over would machine faster but result in a less detailed carving.

With the final pass complete the project is ready for sanding and finishing.

This simple example of the 3-D carving process barely scratches the surface of the work required to create some of the 3-D samples you've seen here from very talented sign makers.

The best way to learn 3-D carving is to start small and work your way up to more complex projects as you gain confidence.

photo by Travis Scott

Begin with some of the abundance of 3-D files available before attempting to learn the complexities of designing and creating your own 3-D models.

2.5-D Signs

When you want to add dimension to your sign without the long 3-D carve times, 2.5-D is the answer.

Without question, dimensional signs catch the viewer's eye in ways no flat sign can. The various layers and textures give depth and create natural shadows. Layers make the sign more interesting, enhance the eye-appeal, and make the sign seem more upscale.

As we've seen, actual 3-D carving has a steep learning curve and requires exceptionally long machine times.

Fortunately there's an alternative: 2.5-D

2.5-D signs add depth by using pocketing toolpaths to make text and artwork appear raised from the background, and to the viewer's eye, mimic 3D carving. The result is a sign with a higher perceived value.

What is 2.5-D?

If we consider a flat sign with v-carved text as 2-D, **adding depth by carving the sign elements at different levels is 2.5-D**.

If you can carve a pocket, you can make a dimensional sign

2.5-D signs just use one or more pockets to raise text and artwork to add dimension. Sometimes, v-carved text is included to add yet another level.

A 2-D sign

A 2.5-D sign

sign by Don Brown, Jr.

raised box for the word "Bar" and a triangle for the words "is open." Then he used a v-carve toolpath to incise the text into the shapes. He also used a subtle visual cue with the triangle pointing to the word "Bar." With the simple use of a pocketing toolpath, Don added life, and value to what would otherwise be a Ho-Hum sign.

Although the artwork is more elaborate, the Fontenot Distillery sign was made the same way.

sign by Tom Hollander

Look at **Don Brown, Jr.'s** sign [The Scruggs]. Had he made a flat v-carved sign using the text and simple silhouettes, he would have had an okay, but a boring sign.

Instead, he pocketed the area around the text and artwork which gave the simple silhouettes dimension. Plus, he added the

Tom Hollander used great shape, and then added another level of dimension by texturing the pocketed area. Texturing also hides tool marks that might require sanding.

You can use a v-bit or a straight bit for your pockets, along with a larger spiral or straight bit to clear the bulk of the pocket.

For texturing, you'll find a ball nose bit works best. Vectric's V-Carve makes it easy to create a wide variety of textures.

Michael Taubitz and Joanne Hibbet used a clever shape and text handling, along with the 2.5-D carving to bring life to the house, and create an engaging sign.

These signs all have one thing in common

Each one has a border. You need an outside vector surrounding the area to be pocketed, otherwise you will just be pocketing the text and art into the surface. The pocketing toolpath will clear out everything between the selected vectors down to whatever you have specified as a cut depth. Cut depths are usually less than 1/4".

sign by Michael Taubitz and Joanne Hibbert
Mike's Custom Unusual

Let's look at this veterinary sign as an example of how to make the toolpaths for a 2.5-D sign. The combined vector of the house and dog, plus the cross were selected, and a pocket toolpath was set using a 1/8" bit at a 0.1" depth of cut. A 1/4" spiral bit cleared the bulk of the area. (The green area.)

For the main body of the sign, the vector for the outside of the house border and the vector for the inside of the main border were selected along with the text vectors to make a pocketing toolpath using a v-bit, and larger clearance area 1/4" spiral bit to cut to a depth of 0.2". That was followed by a texture toolpath with a starting depth of 0.2". (The dark red area.)

sign by Prof. Henry

Using multiple layers and texture

The Chill & Grill sign is carved at three different levels to give it more dimension.

The first level was a pocket around the text vectors to a depth of 0.15". The second pocket was the level of the round frame and the alligator at a depth of 0.30". The final pocket for the alligator's background was 0.50" deep. With the pockets completed, the textures were carved behind the Chill&Grill text and behind the alligator. After that, a profile toolpath cutout the shape.

Here's the best part. The machine time for this sign was only 2.2 hours. A significant saving over 3D.

You can easily see on the unpainted version how the text letters were given an extra layer of dimension by offsetting a vector around the type and pocketing that area outside the letters to make the text raised.

Although the painted alligator looks like it was 3D carved, it's still the same flat shape you see in the raw version. The eye is fooled by adding darker areas of paint in parts of the art to create the appearance of shadows, and give a feeling of roundness.

sign by Prof. Henry

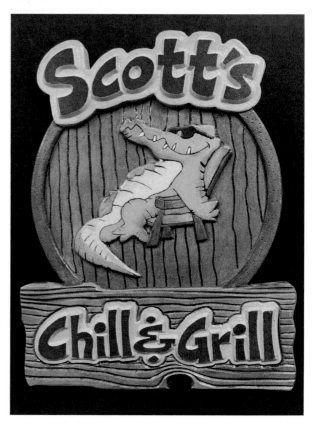

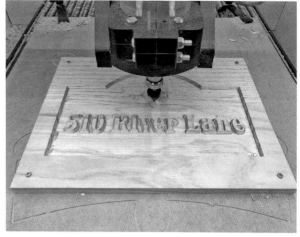

Here's a step-by-step look at making a 2.5-D sign

We'll make the tree and address raised, v-carve the name into the background, and then add a texture. [We're using V Carve.].

Our material is 3/4" thick so let's carve the background around the tree and address down 1/4" using a 60º V-bit.

The start depth is set at 0.0 inches, which is the surface of our material. **The Flat Depth** box is checked and set to 0.25 inches, and we selected the 60º V-bit from our tool database.

Trying to clear out so much material for the background would be time-consuming and challenging with the pointed end of the V-bit, so we can add a **Flat Area Clearance** tool to clear a large area of the flat depth with a flat-bottomed cutter like a 1/4" spiral bit from out Tool Database.

When we save our toolpath, we actually end up with two toolpaths. One for the Flat Area Clearance, and one for the V-carve.

With the pocket for the raised letters and the tree cut using an end mill and V-bit, it's time to set a v-carve toolpath for carving the name into the background with a starting depth of .25" which is the depth of our first carve.

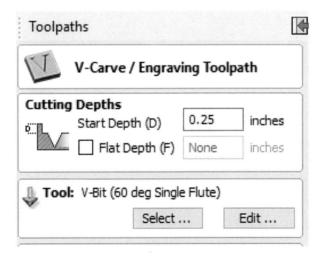

After completing that toolpath, we'll use V Carve's **Texture Toolpath** to quickly add a background texture. Our texture is calculated using the border, tree, and address vectors.

We're using a 1/8" Ball Nose bit from the Tool Database. The start depth is .25" because we're starting at the depth we carved for our background.

A **Boundary Vector Offset** of 0.2" prevents the texture from bumping into and damaging our text, art, or border. Usually, the diameter of the bit is sufficient, but the angle of the v-carved text requires us to leave a little extra room.

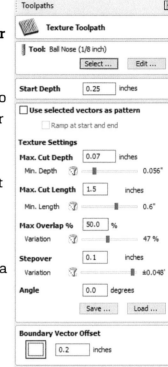

With the texture, toolpath completed it's a simple matter of using a profile toolpath the cut out the outline of the sign, and it's ready for finishing.

That's it! Adding dimension to a sign with 2.5-D carving is that simple.

Stacked text signs

sign by Katie & Jason Loevejoy
Lovejoy Signs - Etsy.com

sign by Darrick Vanderford

Katie and Jason Lovejoy, were trendsetters when they began making stacked text CNC signs around 2009. The technique was quickly adopted by others for wedding, anniversary, and family name gifts, as well as general home decor. **Darrick Vanderford's** sign is another execellent example of the customer-pleasing technique.

Although stacked text signs look look tricky to make, they are actually quite easy to design and machine.

The following layout steps work equally well in Vectric's V Carve, Adobe Illustrator, and Inkscape. Once you have created the proper vectors, machining is easy. We'll use Vectric's V Carve for this example, The other apps work similarly.

Layers are your friend.

Using layers will help you stay organized, and give you a fallback in case things go awry. We need five layers:

- ■ Top Text
- ■ Bottom Text
- ■ Top Text Working
- ■ Bottom Text Working
- ■ Border

You're wondering why we need two layers for the top and bottom text, aren't you?

We're going to be manipulating the text, and **the first two layers are a safety net** to keep them in their original shape in case we need to go back and start over.

Let's get started

1 Create and Name the layers so it will be easy to move things around. Adobe Illustrator and Inkscape layers will work the same way, and keep your work organized.

2 Make the Top Text layer active and type the top text, then COPY it to the Top Text Working layer. We're using the first names for our sample. Almost all Script fonts have some problems that affect how they carve. We'll fix that in a moment. HINT: You should always convert script fonts to outlines.

3 Next, make the Bottom Text layer active and type the bottom text. COPY it to the Bottom Text Working layer. Turn off or hide the Top and Bottom Text Layers. We'll only be using the Top Text Working and the Bottom Text Working layers from here on out. Rembember, those first two layers are just there in case we screw up.

Look carefully, and you can see that the vectors in the script font for the Top Name have overlaps where two letters connect. Most script fonts have those overlapping vectors, and they can cause problems, so we

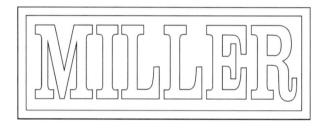

Overlapping vectors

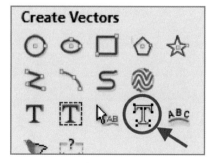

Convert text to curves tool

48 ■ Stacked Text

need to fix them by converting our text from a font to curves or outlines. Use the Convert to Curves Tool in V Carve.

Once your text has been converted to outlines (you can tell it is outlines and selected because it has dotted red lines), DESELECT all of the inner closed areas of each letter. If they are not deselected, they will be lost in the next step.

4 Now that we've created outlines and selected only the outside lines of the word it's time to use the Weld Tool in V Carve (The Unite Tool in Adobe Illustrator) to join the vectors into one piece with no overlaps. The next step is important.

Select all the vectors after welding to include the inside holes of all the letters and GROUP them together as one unit.

The hard part is done. Now you can COPY the welded Top Text to the Bottom Text Working layer.

5 Time for the big finish. Make the Bottom Text Working level the Active level, and select only the Bottom Text word (Miller in our example), and then apply the Create Outlines Tool. With that done, immediately GROUP the vectors.

Since the Bottom Text isn't script we don't have to go through all those actions to Weld overlapping vectors.

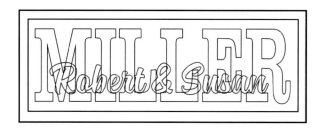

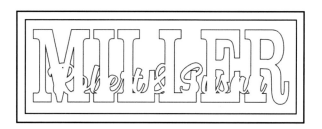

Welded top and bottom text vectors

Okay, we now have two Groups of text on the Bottom Text Working level, the first names and the family name. Select both of them and use the Weld Tool again.

That's it! We have all the vectors we need to make our toolpaths. Now, all that's required are two pocket toolpaths.

For the first pocket, we'll use the Top Text Working vectors and the Border vector.

Let's talk about this Pocket Toolpath for a moment. As you can see we are going to cut to a depth of 0.1 inches, using a .125" end mill.

We're also using a Larger Area Clearance Tool to clear out the bulk of the area. The larger tool dramatically speeds up the over-all carving time.

Note that we're also using a Raster Cut to clear the pocket. The raster cut is going along the x-axis which is the same direction as the grain of our material. Going with the grain helps to hide any tool marks, and can reduce sanding after the carving.

We'll leave the Cutting Depth for the **second toolpath** at 0.1", and we'll be using the vectors on the Bottom Text Working and Border layers.

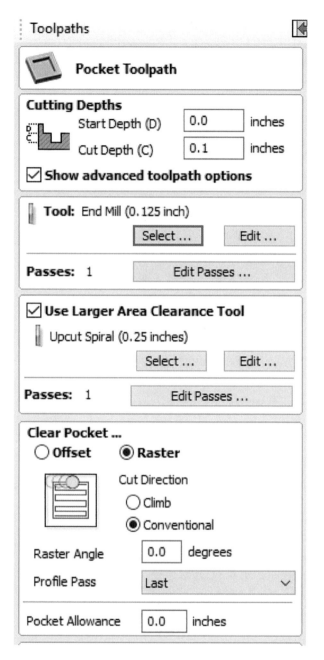

Since we've already carved the top text layer down 0.1" we can set the Bottom Text Start Depth at 0.1" so we don't cut air until it arrives at the level of the first tool path.

You'll now have four tool paths: two larger area clearance paths using a .25" end mill, plus a Top Text and Bottom Text path using a .125" end mill.

You can combine the two larger toolpaths into one file when using your post processor to create the g-code for your machine, and do the same with the two toolpaths for the smaller bit. Having to make only two tool changes saves time.

Here are the results of both the Top Text carving and the Bottom Text carving.

You can see there's no mystery to Stacked Text signs, and they are easier than you thought.

Stacked Text signs are very popular, and some sign makers have trouble keeping up with the demand. **Now that you know how to make them, why don't you give it a go?**

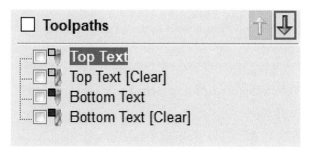

Final tool paths

Top Text layer carved

Bottom Text layer carved

Textures are an easy way to add more depth by creating shadows and making a sign more dramatic.

You can make the texture look like hand chisel marks, woodgrain, cross-hatching, curves, concentric rings, or whatever else you can imagine.

Vectric's V Carve and Aspire products make it very easy to create textures, so we'll use them once again for our demo. Although you may be able to create textures in other software, Vectric has included tools, especially for the purpose.

While generally, the texture is carved into the background, **Jim Hester** amplified the interest by also adding texture to the text of his sign.

sign by Jim Hester

It creates an engaging look and sets the sign apart from other raised text signs.

You can experiment with various vectors to create textures, or if you have a 3-D modeling program, create them from photos of actual textures such as woodgrains and tree bark. Converting high contrast photos of woodgrains to vectors is another way of creating textures for 2D and 2.5D signs.

Psst! Hey you. Can I trust you to keep a secret?

I can? Okay, listen close. See the texture on this sign? It would have taken a long time to make on the CNC, but it was carved in just a few minutes with a 90º bit in a hand-held router.

Everything else was done on the CNC.

You don't have to use your CNC for every sign making operation.

But remember. You didn't hear it from me.

You can learn this background technique at Oldave100 on YouTube.

You can create almost limitless textures, but it can require trial and error in your CAD/CAM program. Textures are easily created with Vectric's V Carve or Aspire software. The texture vectors can be generated by drawing your own, creating them with the Vector Texture tool, or by using the Texture Path tool.

Experiment with different tools to see which works best for your project. Ballnose bits will give a different texture from a V bit, and various V bit angles will also change the look when using the same vectors. All of the textures in following examples were created using a 90º V bit.

This texture uses a 90º V bit to follow a group of vectors drawn vertically, and spaced .25" apart.

This crosshatch texture uses two groups of vectors with the same .25" spacing, and with the first group at a 60º angle, and the second group at 120º.

The 90º V bit was used again to follow vectors created with Vectric's V Carve Vector Texture tool for this woodgrain-like texture.

Vectric V Carve's Texture Toolpath generated a hand-carved-like background still using the 90º bit. A ballnose bit could also be used.

Things were looking good after the large area clearance tool path

Disasters happen, but they aren't all terminal cases.

This project was moving happily along with the large area clearance tool path completed. The end mill was changed to a v-bit for the next step — and then things got ugly.

After a few moments, it was apparent that something was dreadfully wrong with the text in the banner. It was oddly deformed. Stopping the machine and double checking found a 90º v-bit had been used instead of the 60º the toolpath required.

(If you've never made this mistake, don't worry, you will.)

Now what? Is this piece destined for the scrap pile? Maybe not.

Let's see if it can be saved.

Since the v-carve tool path started with the text in the banner, everything else is okay, and we can change to the correct 60º bit, and finish the toolpath.

Now let's fix that text.

First, by going back into the original CAD/CAM program, a new toolpath was created to carve a .25" deep pocket in the banner to clear away the incorrect text.

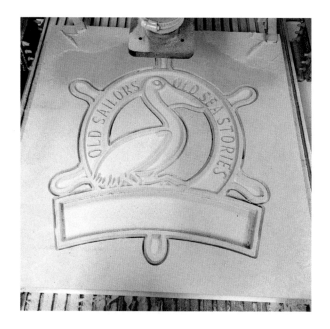

The vectors used to create the pocket and the original text were copied into a new file to carve a patch.

Creating a new vector offset outside the pocket outline ensures the pocket toolpath extends far enough so that there will be a clean edge when cutting along the outside of the pocket vector to cut out the repair part.

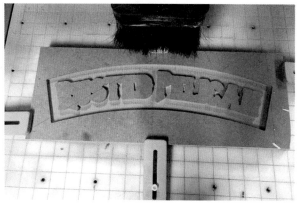

The repair was cut out of 1/2" MDF, and the v-carve toolpath was set to a depth of .25" to leave enough material to match the pocket carved into the sign's banner.

With the pocket carved, the 60º v-bit finished the text so it looked like it should have in the first place.

With the text finished, a simple profile path cut out the repair piece along the pocket's vector, offsetting inward it by .008" to ensure it would fit into the sign's pocket.

After a test fit, the repair piece was glued in place, and the project was saved from the trash bin.

The moral of the story is to be prepared to make mistakes. They happen to everyone.

When you spot your mistake, stop, take a deep breath, and think about ways to fix it.

This sign had a significant error which required major surgery. In many cases, minor bobbles can be repaired with wood putty or epoxy.

If you're painting your sign, the paint may hide the mistake. If staining, a darker stain may help.

Remember you're looking at your sign in close detail while most people will be seeing it at viewing distance which is probably at least six feet away. Small errors and imperfections won't be noticed at that distance.

Bit is too short to cut through blank

Here's a solution for when you don't have an end mill with a cutting length long enough to cut all the way through your material. This project required cutting the outline of the sign through one and a half-inch thick stock, but the bit on hand had only a one-inch cutting length.

The outline vector was cut to a depth of 1/2" with a quarter-inch end mill. Then, the rest of the material was cut away on the bandsaw, leaving a little more than an eighth of an inch of material to be removed.

Next, the router table was set up with a flush-trim bit, with the height set so the bearing rolled along the CNC cut outline, to trim the excess away. A brass starter pin allows you to pivot the work into the bit without worrying about kickback. The job was completed by rounding over the edges with a round-over bit in the table. Sometimes our conventional tools are easier and faster than the CNC.

The router table with a flush-trim bit is also a convenient way to trim tabs created to hold a workpiece together on a through cut out.

section 3

Finishing

W e've been working hard to design and make our signs, and now we're at the second hardest part of sign making.

Finishing.

Mere mortals often cringe at this point because the last thing they want to do is screw up all the work that's been done.

Should the sign be stained, painted, or left natural? What if the stain looks ugly or the paint bleeds into the grain? What about tool marks left behind by the CNC process? What can I do to make the sign look better?

Don't panic. You can do it.

A quick word before we get started. Unless all the stars are aligned and everything about your machine is precise, the tools were right, your speeds and feeds were exceptional, and your material choice impeccable —chances are your sign isn't perfect.

It probably has fuzzies, tool marks, small glitches, and little blemishes that drive you crazy. They can be caused by using an upcut bit on plywood or softwood which makes the edges of the cuts messy, or by a spindle out of tram that leaves tool marks in the bottoms of your pocket cuts.

Whatever the reason, clean up will be required, and it sometimes takes longer than the CNC machining (unless you're a 3D carver.)

You may need a sanding block or a random orbital sander for the large areas. Or perhaps a belt sander or even a surface planer. Plus, a Dremel tool or small hand sanding tools for the detail areas.

And, above all, patience.

Once you've completed the cleanup, you can move on to the real finishing steps of clear coating, staining, or painting.

Detail sanding sticks 80, 120, 180, and 240 grits

CarveWright sanding mop, 180, and 240 grits

Dremel abrasive wheel

It's hard to beat the natural beauty of wood, and often all that's needed is to apply a clear finish that will bring out the details of the grain.

We'll include some stain in this category because many light stains enhance the wood grain without changing the color too much.

sign by Prof. Henry

You'll find that flooding the carved areas with the finish, such as the amber shellac on the Stan's Bee's sign, actually adds color, depth, and contrast. The natural finish reinforces the natural product.

Cris Hinojosa's American flag has contrast in the stars and bars even without adding the expected red, white, and blue colors.

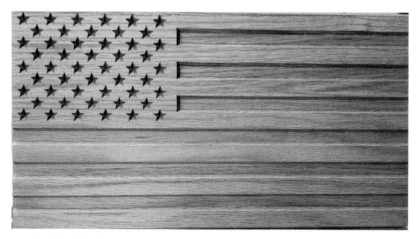

sign by Cris Hinojosa

You can always give your sign a natural finish to start and then add color later if you think it needs it.

sign by Tom Hollander

Don't underestimate the power of adding color to your signs. Color can add a lot of eye candy to any sign. Paint can be a basic single-color monochrome that adds contrast to the natural wood background or multiple colors that support and enhance the message.

Tom Hollander carved his sign out of poplar and hand-painted with acrylic paints for an almost photographic look when viewed from a distance.

Color can effectively connect different parts of your overall message to give your sign a sense of completeness and unity.

Both **Gary Wiant** and **Grant Davis** used color effectively to give their signs a lot of visual appeal.

sign by Grant Davis

Grant used red for the maple leaf outline and the word Union on his sign, subliminally establishing the location of Local 269.

The color makes the artwork on Gary's sign pop and the touch of red in the hog's shirt ties it to the red in the main headline to unify all the sign's elements.

sign by Gary Wiant

Lee Cowan's sign is a terrific example of what can be easily done with paint to make a sign that grabs your attention. Here's how he painted his sign.

"The painting was super easy. The sign is cedar and had some uneven tones to the wood. I sprayed on Kilz stain block primer. Then the base coat was also sprayed on with a little brushing to make sure I covered all the tight spots.

All the raised portions were painted with a 6" foam roller. Roll the roller in the paint, do a little roll on a scrap piece to make sure it won't drip, then lightly roll over the high spots on the sign. It literally took just a few minutes, and the results were great, even a beginner can pull off a slick paint job.

The paint I used is Behr Premium Ultra from Home Depot. I used two coats of paint, and I'm delighted with the results."

Lee's sign is also an excellent example of why you don't need to stress out about painting your signs. As you can see, painting isn't a big deal.

After all, it's just paint. If you mess up badly, give it another coat of primer and start again. In the end, no one will know how many times you painted. They'll only see the final result and an excellent sign.

sign by Lee Cowan

If you want the **absolute easiest way** to add color to a sign, this is it, and it is virtually fool-proof.

It works best for simple v-carved designs, but you could experiment with small pocketed areas also to see if you like the look.

The technique could not be more uncomplicated. Just pre-paint your material with the color of your choice. Clamp it in place on the CNC table, and carve. The carved areas show as the natural color of the material, so the only thing you have to plan for is enough contrast between the paint and your base material,

When the carving is done —you're done. All that is needed is a clear coat finish to seal the carved areas. It's an easy way to crank out a lot of signs in a short time.

If you're making a lot of the similar-sized signs, you could pre-paint a larger sheet, gang the artwork up on the large piece, carve, and then cut the signs to size.

This Cigar & Whiskey Bar sign was carved with a single 90º v-bit, so no tool changes were required, and the cutting time was very short.

Carve / Paint / Sand / Finish

sign by Patrick Eaton

Without a doubt, the fastest and most common way to paint the carved areas of v-carved signs is to use spray paint or a brush to fill in the carved letters without worrying about neatness. After the paint dries, the entire surface is sanded to remove the excess paint from the sign's surface, leaving only the carved areas painted.

Patrick Eaton used the carve/paint/sand technique to make his beautiful redwood sign, and the black color provides an excellent contrast to the natural wood background. A final clear topcoat finish brings out the wood grain and color.

Flat primer paint in rattle spray cans works well with this method because it dries quickly, gives good coverage, and sands easily. Use a light touch when spraying, so you don't get too much on the surface. The darker color will add the contrast you need even if the paint coverage inside the carved areas is thin.

This technique is especially helpful when you are making a large number of signs, such as for craft shows or online sales, where speed-of-production is critical.

Carve the sign

Apply the paint

Sand away the excess paint

Seal before painting

sign by Cade Banks

You may encounter a common problem when you are using paint or even epoxy to fill your carved text and art. With some woods, particularly softer ones like pine, the paint or other fill material wants to bleed into the grain and can make the letters look blurry.

Remember, once you have carved into the surface, all the cut portions become end grain and can act like a sponge, soaking up the paint. The solution is to seal the carving with shellac, wood sealer, or a polyurethane finish before applying paint or other filler.

The sealer can be either sprayed or brushed on, as long as you get a heavy enough coat to ensure the surface is well sealed.

Sealing the surface will also help reduce trapped bubbles when using epoxy coatings and fillers.

Although woods like redwood and cedar don't have the bleeding problems and won't need the sealers, it is a good idea to test your material before committing to painting your finished sign and risking all of your work.

Sealing softwoods before carving can also help minimize tear out, particularly on small text.

Bullseye 1-2-3 water-based primer works well as a base coat for signs that will be entirely painted , particularly on porous materials like MDF.

Paint by number

There is often a full-color version available when using vector clip art, and it is an easy guide to painting the artwork you used on your sign.

Unless you've got artistic talent, the ability to copy well, and a steady hand, the color rendering probably isn't going to help you much,

There's an easy way to replicate the artwork.

Set up a tool path like a paint by numbers coloring book. The separate tool path, using a narrow-angled v-bit or engraving bit that follows the detail vectors of your artwork will give you a comfortable and stress-free way of painting.

The carved lines give your brush a real stopping point when it gets close to an edge, and prevents you from slopping paint over into the next section. You can fill the carved guidelines with contrasting paint before applying the colors, or let them fill with glaze after painting.

Masking makes painting simple

If you don't have a steady hand, and sometimes nerves of steel, painting your signs can be a tedious, stressful experience. It can also slow your production to a crawl as you spend an excessive amount of time finishing your sign.

We've looked at some of the simpler methods of adding color to a sign, but what if you want more colors and more details?

Masking can help.

Jason Herrman's and **Jeff Schumacher's** signs show how effective the masking technique is for adding color. Jason painted his sign white before masking, while Jeff masked the natural wood.

Masking is the application of a covering over the sign blank which you then carve through. You paint the carved areas, after cutting, and before removing the mask. The mask works like a stencil to give you a perfectly painted sign without worrying about staying within the lines.

Removing the mask is called "weeding," and you can see from Jeff's photo that it can take a while to pick-away all the small pieces of masking.

The most popular masking material is a vinyl product called Oramask 813. Its

sign by Jason Herrman

sign by Jeff Schumacher

transparency makes it easy to position and has just enough stickiness to stick to the base coat without lifting it off or pulling up wood fibers when removed. Other materials like shelf covering and blue painter's tape can also be used as a mask.

Here are the steps to successfully using the masking technique.

- Prepare the surface using 180 or 220 grit sandpaper. A smooth surface is needed for the mask.

- For a solid background color, pre-paint with the color of choice, or seal with a few coats of shellac or other clear finish for a natural background.

- Lightly sand the painted/sealed surface with a Scotch-Brite™ pad or 200 grit sandpaper to eliminate any bumps.

- Apply the masking film and smooth with a roller or squeegee for good adhesion.

- Carve the sign through the mask

- For materials like MDF, it helps to seal the carved area with shellac before painting.

- Paint the carved areas either with spray or by hand.

- Weed away the masking material, and give the sign a final clear coat of finish.

Weeding the mask can be tedious. Use caution if using a sharp-pointed tool like an Exacto knife for lifting the edge of the mask. You may accidentally scrape or chip the background paint.

Trevor Viner's step-by-step photos below show how masking makes painting v-carved signs quick and stress-free.

sign by Trevor Viner - trevslittlewoodshop.com

Masked sign after carving

Sign spray painted with two colors

Final sign with masking film removed

Other ways to add color to your signs

Paint and stain aren't the only way you can add color to your sign. You can explore other options by experimenting on scraps of wood, or whichever material you use for your signs.

For this welcome sign, the background was painted with a rattle spray can of brown primer, then the surface was sanded to remove the paint from the top surface.

The color was added to the alligator with permanent felt tip markers, which are easy to apply and come in a wide range of colors. A light wash of stain followed by a clear seal coat completed the sign.

Another technique worth testing is using oil pastels from the art or craft store to apply color to the sign.

Like the markers, oil pastels come in a wide range of colors and are as easy to use as the crayons you had as a kid. The colors can be applied singly or layered to create a new color.

Rubbing the area with a finger after applying the pastels, will smooth, and blend the color onto the sign.

Sealing the surface with Shellac or another clear finish and lightly sanding, will make it easier to apply and smooth the pastels.

An antique, worn effect can be achieved by not thoroughly blending the pastels when applying, as you can see on this sign.

Special Painting Techniques

This collaboration by **Mark Taylor** and **David Tolley** uses paint to give an authentic antique feel to the sign.

Mark first put down a base layer of primer to seal the wood, and then built up the paint in several layers, rubbing it back in places for a weathered appearance.

After completing the painting, he top-coated everything with a watered down dark varnish, which clings to the crevices and gives it a dirty 'used' look. He added a drop shadow under the word Invités with metallic gold paint.

Sign design and paint by Mark Taylor
CAD/CAM and CNC by David Tolley

Branwen Cole uses a dry brush technique to add a weathered effect to the background boards of her sign.

She applied the whitewash by using barely any paint on the brush and then adding a touch of water to thin it further.

The dry brush technique can be used with multiple colors to build depth and interest to painted pieces.

sign by Branwen Cole

Glazing

Glazing is an excellent technique for adding depth to a painted sign. The glaze provides shading and antiquing effects, by adding a thin transparent or semi-transparent layer of color onto the surface and changing the appearance of the underlying paint layer. Glazes are thin because there is a large amount of binding medium and a minimal amount of pigment. You can buy clear glaze and tint it with your paint to make your own glazes.

Glazing works well on semi-gloss or low-luster acrylic or latex paint surfaces. Flat paints can be sealed with a quick coat of shellac for polyurethane, and you can apply glaze after the top coat has completely dried. Raw wood needs to be sealed with shellac or another sealer before using any glazes.

When you paint your sign with simple colors, you can use the glaze's transparency to build up multiple layers in different shades to significantly enhance the depth, and add richness to your colors. Glazing can also be used to add effects like wood grain to non-wood surfaces like HDU and MDF.

Before applying glaze

The colors look richer after applying glaze

You apply glaze by brushing over the entire area, making sure to gets deep into carved areas, corners, and textures. It is not quite as thick as a gel stain, but begins to set up fairly quickly,

After a few moments wipe the excess with a shop towel or rag, rubbing to remove as much as possible in areas where you want the original finish to show, and lightly where you want the glaze to stay.

You need to work reasonably quickly when using glaze and may want to keep a rag in one hand and a brush in the other when applying glaze to a large area.

The oak Fontenot Distillery sign lacked contrast with stain alone, making it difficult to read the small text from a distance.

sign by Prof. Henry

By applying burnt umber glaze and letting it sit in the deeper carvings, the text became legible, and the sign achieved a pleasing overall patina.

Paul E. Wilson uses a glazing-like technique for finishing. He applies stain and lets it stand for about a half an hour, and then wipes the top surface with denatured alcohol to remove some of the stain and lighten the color, leaving the deeper carved areas untouched. The contrast between dark and light areas add dimension.

sign by Paul E. Wilson
WilsonsCreatiions – Facebook

Justin Walsh uses a clever technique to stain the tops of the letters and the carved 3D art on his projects, without getting any on the background.

Trying to stain the text and letters after carving would require careful, tedious work. Justin carves the outlines of his text, border, and the 3D element. Then he stains the surface of the wood without removing the work from the spoilboard.

After the stain has dried, he resumes the job and carves away the background, leaving the dark text against the light wood background, which can then be finished with a clear topcoat.

His technique significantly reduces finishing time while creating a distinctive final product.

sign by Justin Walsh

Gary Wiant uses a technique similar to Justin's when he wants to pre-paint his signs before carving.

For this sign, made from 1" thick PVC, Gary primed the board with Sherwin William's Extreme Bond Primer and then used a 1/8" bit to route an outline about 1/2" to 3/4" outside of the edges of his letters. The outline serves as a guide for where to paint, almost like paint-by-number.

With the sign blank still in place on the CNC, he painted it with three coats of Sherwin Williams acrylic paint, using the shallow carved outlines as a guide. When the paint was dry, he carved the sign with a 1/4" end mill to a depth of about 0.4" around the text and logo before cutting out the sign's outline.

The sign was complete and ready for delivery as it came off of the machine.

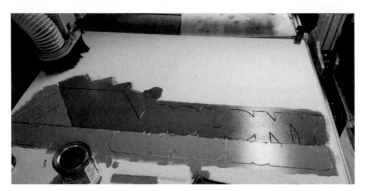

sign by Gary Wiant

Faux Finishes

sign by Prof. Henry

sign by Bob Mary Walters

Faux finish techniques can make your sign look like it is made from a completely different material than it actually is.

This old, rusted-looking sign isn't metal at all. It is actually MDF finished with **Sculpt Nouveau's Iron B metal coating** which has ground metal suspended in a non-toxic water-based acrylic binder.

They are easily brushed on, and once dry, the coating is hard enough to be burnished with steel wool to adjust the highlights. The metal coatings are suitable for outdoor use and are very durable for 10–15 years.

The metal coatings from **Sculpt Nouveau** and **Modern Masters** come in a variety of finishes including Iron, Brass, Copper, Bronze, Pewter, and Silver.

Bob Mary Walters used flat Sherwin Williams exterior paint, and **Sculpt Nouveau Brass B** for the badge on his elegant sign. He also used One Shot Black for the black in the badge.

Let's take a look at the Pelican sign to see how the process works

First, the MDF was given a couple of coats of shellac to seal it, and then it was primed with **Rust-Oleum Rusty Metal primer**. The primer already gives it a bit of a rusted look and makes an excellent base for the metal coating.

The Iron B paint is applied in two coats. The first coat is allowed to dry for about an hour, and while the second coat is still wet, Sculpt Nouveau's green patina is spritzed onto the sign. In just a few minutes, the acidic patina begins to rust the iron particles in the paint.

If you aren't satisfied with the results, you can rub it down with steel wool to expose the iron particles, and reapply the patina.

After 12 hours give the sign a top coat of clear finish to prevent the iron from rusting further.

In addition to the iron, the Tiffany Green patina works on the bronze, brass, and copper coatings.

As you can see, the results are amazing.

[Although the metal coating is weatherproof, this MDF sign was intended for indoor use only.]

Painting insulation foam

You would never suspect **Casey Reames** carved this sign out of inexpensive 2" thick pink insulation foam from the big box store. While the insulation foam is not as dense as the HDU typically used for sign making and requires some extra finishing work, it works surprisingly well for test carves and interior decor items.

sign by Casey Reames

Casey said when first carved, the insulation foam looks pretty bad. However brushing off the loose fuzz, and then going over it very lightly with a heat gun melts the rest of the fuzzies and smooths out the surface. The melted fuzz brushes right off After heating.

Casey used Rust-Oleum Foam Primer, which allows the foam to be painted with aerosol paints without damage. Otherwise, the oil-based aerosol paints melt the foam when applied.

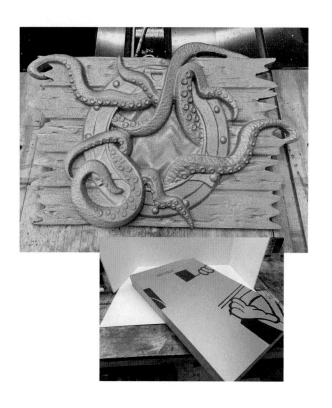

To finish the sign he first gave the white primer an overall coat of Rust-Oleum Metallic, Aged Copper, and then faded in Rust-Oleum Black Stainless Steel by going back and forth, spraying the two colors at different angles until he was satisfied with the look.

Commercial sign makers often use printed vinyl elements combined with CNC carved letters and backgrounds on large sign installations when they need to add something with a lot of detail.

You can apply the same technique on a smaller scale, even if you don't have a vinyl printer. Particularly for indoor signage.

The pirate artwork in this sign is way too complicated for hand-painting by most mere mortals, so it required another approach.

The solution was to print the artwork on a laser or inkjet printer and embed it on the sign with ModPodge after carving and painting. Although paper was used on this sign, letter-size inkjet-compatible vinyl is available.

The sign was designed in Vectric's V Carve with the artwork as the focal point, and as with most designs, it required finagling to decide how large it should be. The size of the pirate was crucial because both the tool paths and sizing and cutting out the artwork needed the same size vector outline.

One of the advantages of working with vector artwork in V Carve is the ability to trans-

Preparing to cut out the artwork

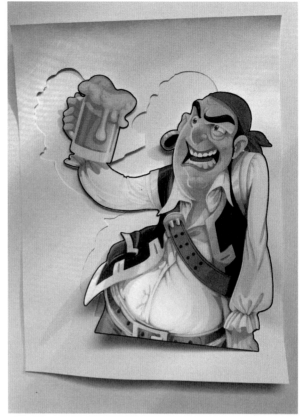

The artwork cut out and ready for the sign

fer the vectors back and forth with other applications.

With the pirate's size established on the V Carve sign layout, the artwork was resized in Adobe Illustrator for printing.

After the artwork was printed, it was cut out with an electronic craft cutting machine. In this case, the ScanNCut device which can scan the artwork and create an outline cutting vector.

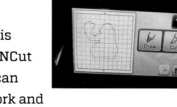

The process was made easier by applying a thicker black border to the artwork in Adobe Illustrator. You can do the same with any vector-based art software or by hand with a felt-tipped marker.

Don't despair if you don't have a cutting machine. You can always cut out artwork with the old standby Exacto knife.

The Pirate art was cut out several times by hand during the design process to help visualize sizes. The trick to hand cutting

Cheat with an Applique ■ 79

Testing the fit

Sign painting complete and ready for art installation

is to relax and take it slow. The more tense your hand, the less accurate your cuts, and it is usually easier to cut towards yourself rather than away.

After cutting, a quick check showed the V Carve vector, and the artwork outline was a perfect match.

A few coats of spray shellac on both sides will seal any paper before attaching it to a project.

With the artwork prepared, the sign was sealed with shellac and hand painted, before appliquéing the art in position with ModPodge. The artwork could as easily have been attached with spray glue, or in the case of vinyl, with its own sticky back.

You may find this technique useful for other items like this quick little wall decor.

Frame it

sign by Teresa Carson

sign by Robert Peloat

Frames are a fast way to make a sign look complete and add a sense of substance.

Teresa Carson's beautiful v-carved sign hits all the marks for simple, yet elegant sign production. The wreath-wrapped monogram serves as a focal point, and the addition of the frame gives it the look of finished work, instead of a just being a flat rectangle.

The dark frame around **Branwen Cole's** sign helps focus the eye inward towards the matching color name. The stark contrast gives the sign a contemporary vibe.

The textured border on **Robert Peloat's** sign is equally effective at framing the central artwork, and if stained, would add additional contrast.

sign by Branwen Cole
On the Wall Designs

Materials & Supplies

There are as many choices for sign making materials and supplies as there are talented sign makers, and making a comprehensive list is impossible.

But if you aren't sure where to begin or want to explore other options, the following pages have information you may find helpful.

One cautionary note: the Internet changes rapidly and any web addresses listed may have changed since publication. A web search should help you find what you need.

Materials

Hardwoods

Photo: Wood-Database.com

Hardwoods make beautiful signs because they hold fine detail well, and look good when finished with stain, oil, or clear finishes. Close-grained woods like cherry, birch, maple, and walnut hold small detail, and work well for both v-carves and 3-D carves Oak will v-carve well but may be too grainy for good 3-D carvings.

Pros
- Standard wood finishes
- Easy to paint and stain
- Carves cleanly
- Generally fine, straight grain

Cons
- Can be expensive
- May warp and crack

Softwoods

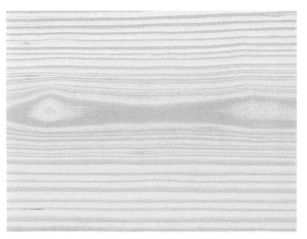

Photo: Wood-Database.com

Softwoods like pine, redwood, cedar, and cypress, are easy to machine and carve. Although poplar is technically a hardwood, it fits in this category also. You may experience tear-out, especially in pine, which can be alleviated by using down cut bits for some operations. Tear out can be reduced by applying wood sealer or shellac to the surface before carving. Stains may blotch without a pre-treatment.

Pros
- Generally inexpensive
- Standard wood finishes
- Easy to paint
- Stable

Cons
- Edges tend to fuzz
- Tear out common
- Wide grain

Medium Density Fiberboard (MDF)

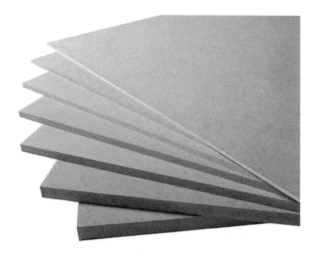

Baltic Birch Plywood

Photo: Wood-Database.com

MDF is used for a lot of signs because it carves easily, paints well, and is flat, and dimensionally stable. Readily available in thicknesses from 1/4" — 1". The manufactured product has no wood grain , no knots, and no voids.

Pros
- Uniformly smooth
- Easily machined
- Easy to paint
- Dimensionally stable

Cons
- Breathing MDF sawdust is hazardous
- Heavy
- Does not take stain well
- Not weather resistant
- Thin carved areas can be weak and prone to break

When working with plywood, the best choice is Baltic Birch. It isn't a specific species but represents wood from Russia, Finland, and other Baltic countries.

Baltic Birch, or BB as it is often called, is made entirely from birch plies with no softwood fillers. It has about double the number of plies found in most other plywoods and generally is void-free. The additional plies add stiffness and stability.

Pros
- Uniformly flat surfaces
- Generally void-free
- Face veneers thicker than found on big box store plywood sheets
- Sands well
- Stainable

Cons
- Large sheet size is 5' x 5'
- Like other plywoods, may have oval shaped patches on the surfaces.
- Pricier than standard birch plywood

High Density Urethane (HDU)

Photo: Coastal Enterprises – PrecisionBoard.com

HDU has many advantages. The best may be that it carves easily and holds crisp detail. It is lightweight and impervious to weather, making it perfect for outdoor signage. Usually only available in large sheets, and pricey. Can be difficult to find locally.

HDU is sold in densities ranging from 4—75 lbs. Density is the weight of one cubic foot of material, and the weights most commonly used for signs are 15 to 20 lb. HDU goes by many names including, Precision Board, Sign-Foam, and Corafoam.

Pros
- Very easy to carve
- Holds detail well
- Lasts up to 10 times longer than wood
- Weatherproof
- Easy to paint

Cons
- Expensive
- Hard to get in cut sizes
- Large spans need extra support
- Susceptible to scratches and dings

Polyvinyl Chloride (PVC)

PVC comes in typical 4' x 8' sheets and some larger, in varying thicknesses from 1/4" up to 1-1/4". It cuts and machines easily and can be painted with most paints. As with HDU, little tiny static charged chips stick to everything. It can be glued with the same PVC cement used to connect PVC pipes.

Available in colors, but they may fade when used outdoors.

Pros
- Easy to machine
- Easy to paint
- Weatherproof
- Excellent for cut out letters and words

Cons
- May expand in hot weather
- Susceptible to scratches and dings
- Difficult to sand
- Static-charged chips stick to everything.

Router bits

You don't need a lot of bits to get started on your sign making journey. You can begin making signs with only two or three essential bits: a 90º v-bit, a 60º v-bit, and a 1/4" upcut spiral end mill.

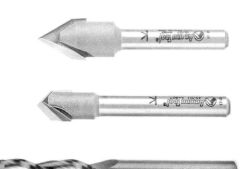

As you progress, you'll start adding more v-bits like 45º and smaller to let you cut deeper in smaller text, smaller end mills so you can clear out tighter areas more precisely, and, perhaps some down-cut spiral end mills so you can eliminate tear-out on the top surface of your cuts.

Wider v-bits, such as a 120º, will help prevent a full depth v carve from cutting too deeply into large text. If you are making a lot of cutouts of letters and words from plywood or MDF, a compression bit will help you get cuts with smooth edges on both the top and bottom surfaces.

For 3D work, you'll need ball nose bits in various sizes. The smaller the ball nose, the more detail you can achieve when cutting your 3D model. But remember, the smaller the ball nose bit, the longer the carving time.

Router bit photos © Amana Tool Corporation

Router bits are available in a range of prices, and the quality is pretty much directly proportional. Some top brands are Amana, Whiteside, Freud, and CMT.

Brad nailers

In addition to router bits, there are some other useful tools you should consider. A pneumatic brad nailer will help hold sign elements in place while glue sets or hold you work in place on the spoilboard.

Composite brad nailer

New plastic polymer composite fasteners can be a useful addition to your tool lineup. The composite fasteners can be sanded, shaped, and cut without damage to router bits, cutting blades or sanding belts. Multiple pieces of material can be stacked and attached to the spoil board with the composite fasteners, eliminating the need to use metal screws or other hold-downs.

The fasteners have low shear strength. All that is needed is a sharp rap with a mallet against one edge of the stock to break the composite fastener at the point between the stock and spoilboard when machining is complete.

The composite fasteners require a special brad nailer like the one from Senco.

23 gauge Pin Nails

In addition to standard 16 or 18 gauge brad nailers, a 23 gauge pin nailer is a beneficial addition to your arsenal. It is particularly helpful if you are making signs with stacked elements from thinner materials like 1/4" plywood or MDF.

The headless, pin-like brass brads are almost invisible when in place. Since they are so small, there is virtually no chance of splitting the wood. They are an excellent solution for holding pieces in place while the glue dries.

Finish sprayer

An inexpensive air-powered siphon spray gun, like this one from Critter, will spray stain, lacquer, paint, or other finishes.

Clean-up is fast and easy as the liquid is drawn directly from the reservoir and does not flow through the gun. Best of all, it uses any size of standard Mason jar as the reservoir for easy storage of paints or finishes without having to clean a paint cup or buy expensive extras.

Adhesives and glues

You will invariably need glue when making your signs, particularly for cut-and-stacked signs or making larger panels by edge-gluing narrow stock.

There is a wealth of information available on the merits of one type of adhesive vs. another. Here is just a brief overview of some of the adhesives useful for sign making.

PVA (polyvinyl acetate) glues from manufacturers like Titebond® and Elmers®, are water-based, making them easy to use. Once set, PVA glue is water-resistant, and in the case of Titebond III®, waterproof. Squeeze out, tools, and hands can be easily cleaned up with water. PVA glues are the most common choice for wood.

Polyurethane glues like Gorilla Glue® or Titebond® Polyurethane work well for wood and are the glue of choice for HDU (high-density urethane). The glue is waterproof when cured. Squeeze out can be cleaned up with mineral spirits or acetone before it cures. Wear gloves to keep it off your skin

CA (Cyanoacrylate) glue (commonly called super glue) is a strong, quick bonding glue that works on a wide variety of substrates. Some versions like products from FastCap and Starbond use a spray accelerator to reduce the CA bonding time to a matter of

seconds. CA glues are best used for applying small applique´s, rather than edge bonding or other joints that will be stressed.

Epoxy makes a strong bond between a variety of materials. It is a two-part adhesive that requires mixing a resin with a hardener. Poured poxy can also be used to fill carved areas, and as a high gloss, final overall sealing finish.

PVC glue is the same stuff used to glue PVC pipes for plumbing and is the only glue that will work well when gluing PVC sign elements together.

	PVA	POLY	CA	EPOXY	PVC
WOOD	✔	✔	✔	✔	
MDF	✔	✔	✔	✔	
HDU		✔		✔	
PVC				✔	✔

Adhesive recommendations

Paints and finishes

This is by no means a comprehensive list, but it will give you a good starting point if you aren't sure where to find the paint or finish you need beyond what is usually found in the big box stores.

Links can change quickly, so an internet search may be required.

1Shot Paints: oil-based, high gloss enamels for interior and exterior use on metal, wood or glass with vibrant colors and durability
www.1shot.com

Coastal Enterprises: Primers, hard coat, and texture finishes for HDU board
www.precisionboard.com

Createx Colors: water-based airbrush Colors made with lightfast pigments and acrylic resin. Available in transparent, opaque, fluorescent and pearlized colors.
www.createxcolors.com

Crystalac: high gloss acrylic and polyurethane waterborne finishing products, metallics, wood sealers, and grain fillers
www.thecrystalacstore.com

General Finishes: chalk paint, water-based stains & dyes, glazes, and top coats
www. generalfinishes.com

Matthews Paint: primers, paints, and clear finishes
www.matthewspaint.com

Modern Masters: water-based metallics, flat solid colors, and dead-flat varnish with UV blockers
www.modernmasters.com

Nova Color Paints: water-based acrylic paints with high pigment content
www.novacolorpaint.com

Sign Arts Products Corp.: Primer for HDU board
www.signfoam.com

Sculpt Nouveau: textured, specialty metallic, and patina finishes
www.sculptnouveau.com

Sherwin Williams Co: Base coat/clear coat paint system and single-stage finishes
www.sherwin-williams.com

Fonts and artwork

Fonts

Both free and paid fonts are readily available for download and use in your sign designs. Paid fonts have glyphs (fancy special characters), complete punctuation characters, and multi-language support that generally are not found in free fonts.

Free Fonts
- 1001freefonts.com
- AbstractFonts.com
- Befonts.com
- Dafont.com
- Fontspace.com
- Fontsquirrel.com
- Urbanfonts.com

Paid Fonts
- Creativemarket.com
- Envatoelements.com
- Fonts.adobe.com
- Fontbundles.net
- Graphicriver.net
- Letterheadfonts.com
- Myfonts.com

Vector art

Your artwork must be vector format for your CNC sign making, and you can generally find an online source for vector artwork that can be adapted for your sign. You may need to node edit downloaded vector artwork for proper machining.

Free Vector Art
- 123FreeVectors.com
- Freedesignfile.com
- Freevector.com
- Vecteezy.com
- Retrovectors.com
- Vectorportal.com

Paid Vector Art
- graphicpear.com
- graphicriver.net
- Vectorstock.com

*Many of the free vector sites also have vectors that can be purchased individually or as part of a subscription.

Made in the USA
San Bernardino, CA
10 March 2020